EXTREME MAZES

BY DR GARETH MOORE

B.Sc (Hons) M.Phil Ph.D

Take on the ultimate maze challenge and solve the fiendishly tricky labyrinths in this book. There are mazes of different types, shapes, sizes and difficulties to pit your wits against. Here are some of the challenges you will meet:

Bridge mazes

- These puzzles include bridges. Bridges allow your solution path to cross over and under itself. This example shows how bridges work. Beware – they can make a maze trickier to solve, and it's much easier to miss a potential route.

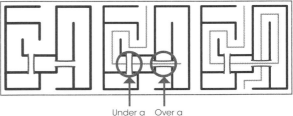

Under a bridge   Over a bridge

Warp mazes

- These puzzles are similar to multi-floor mazes, but warp mazes are contained within a single grid. They contain letters which act as portals – but there are multiple options of where you can 'warp' to.

- When you reach a letter in a warp maze, look for other letters that are the same. You can choose to continue your path at any of the same letters, or you can ignore the portals and carry on past – the choice is yours. Just watch out for dead ends!

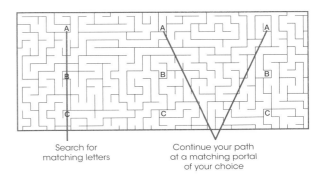

Search for matching letters

Continue your path at a matching portal of your choice

Michael O'Mara Books Limited

Start

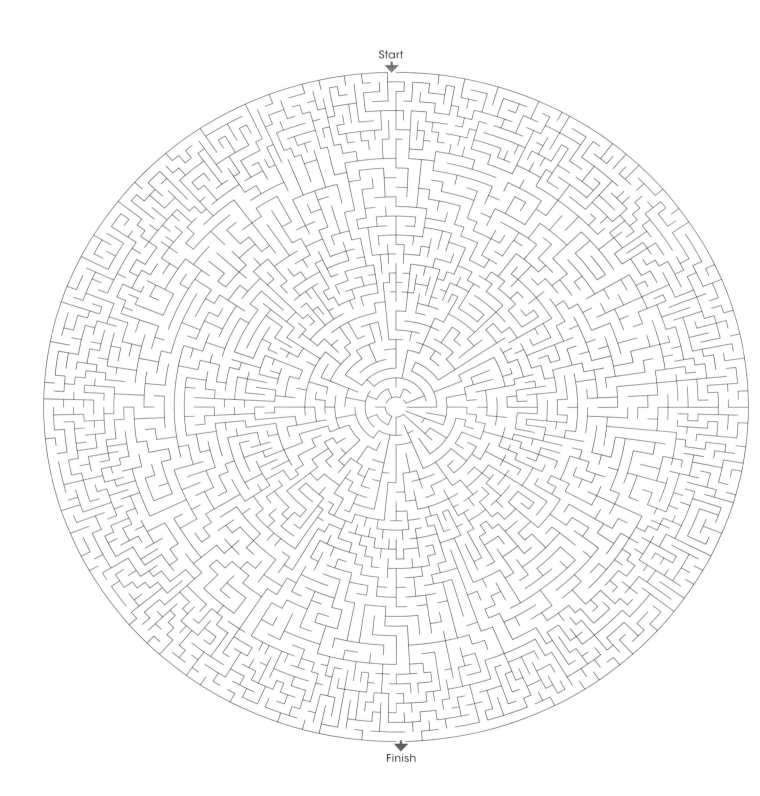

Finish

Start

Finish

Start

Finish

Start

Finish

Start

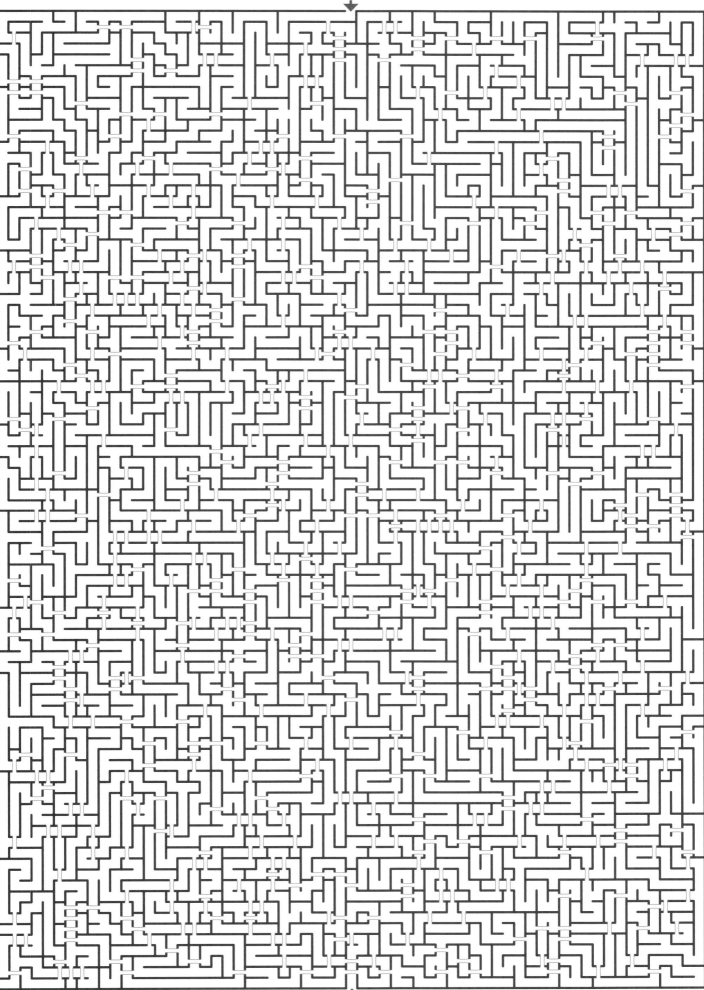

Finish

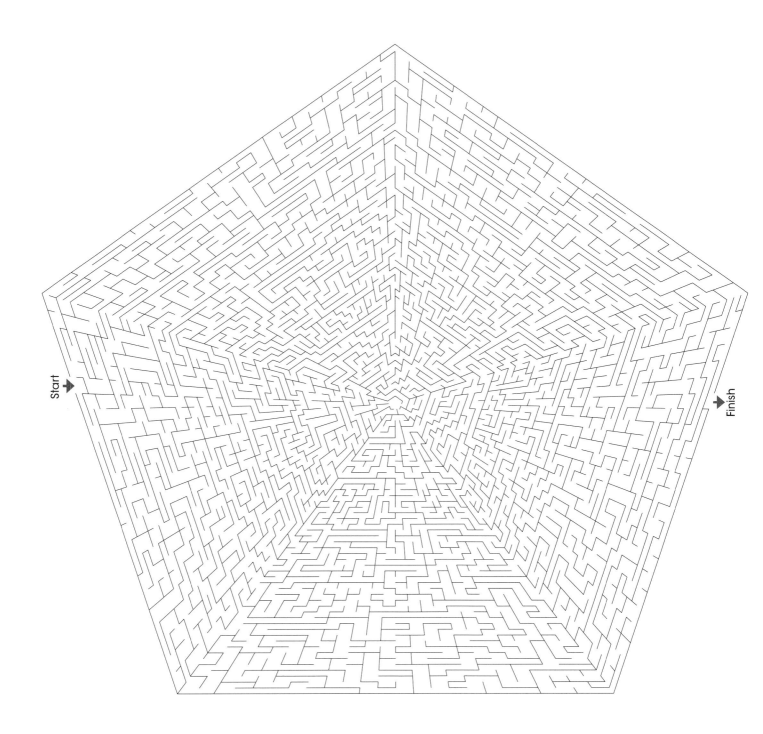

Start ➤

Finish ➤

Start

Finish

Start

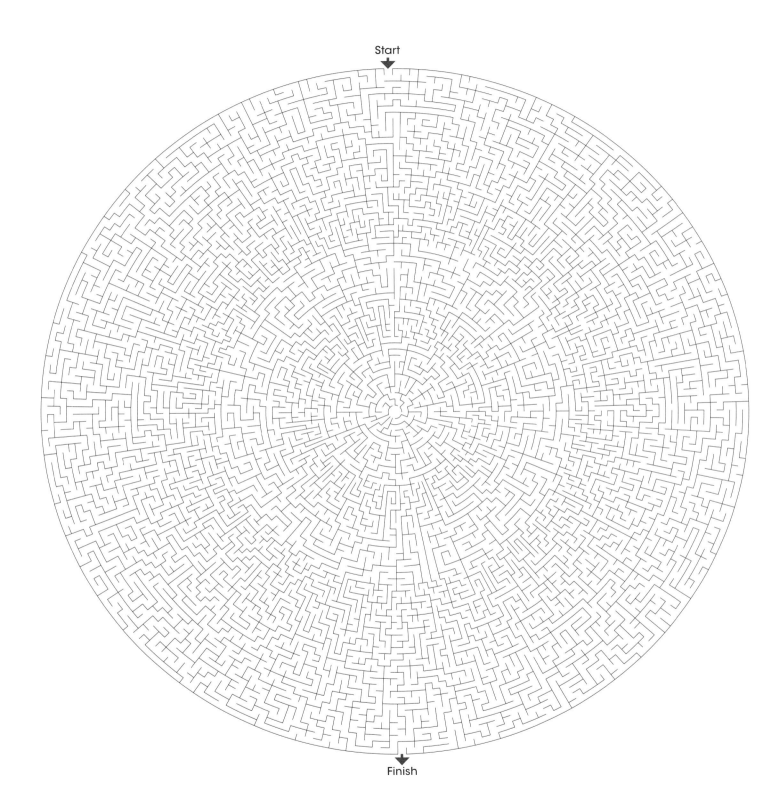

Finish

Start

Finish

Start

Finish

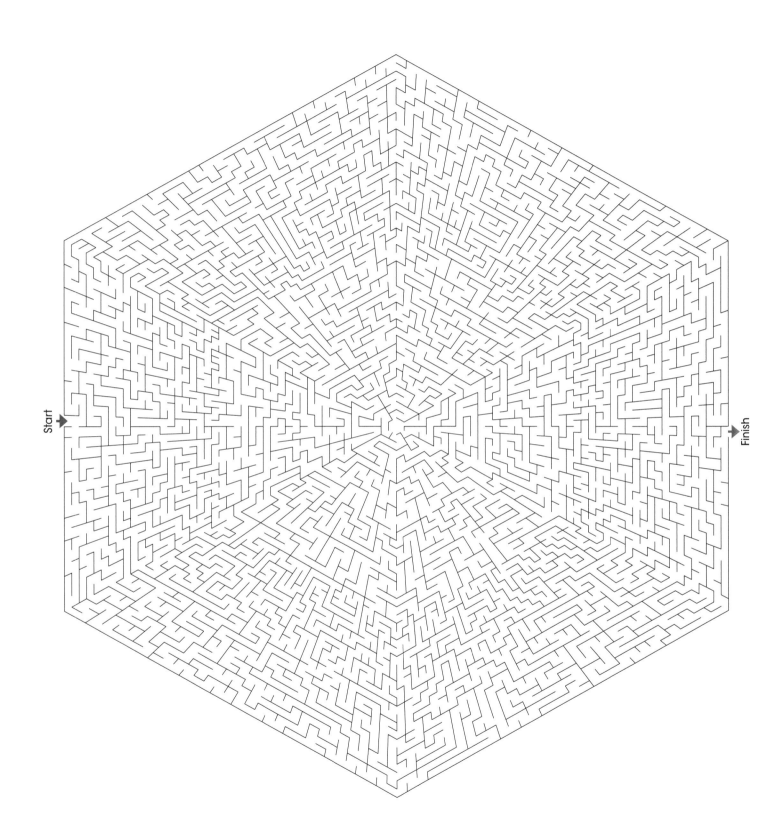

Start

Finish

Start

Finish

Start

Finish

Start

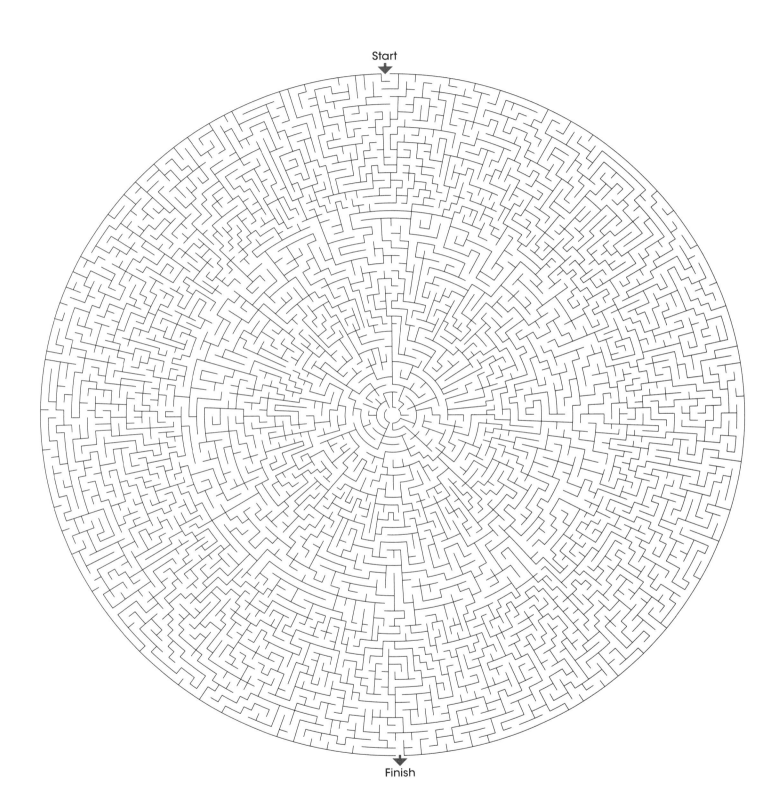

Finish

Finish

Start

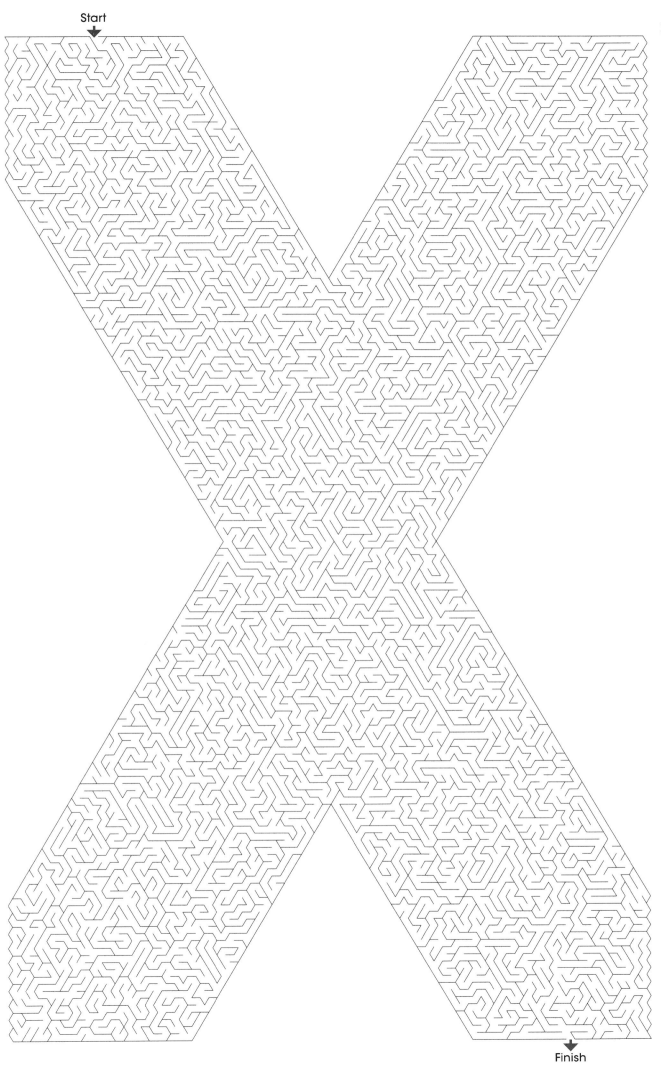

Finish

Start

Finish

Start

Finish

Start

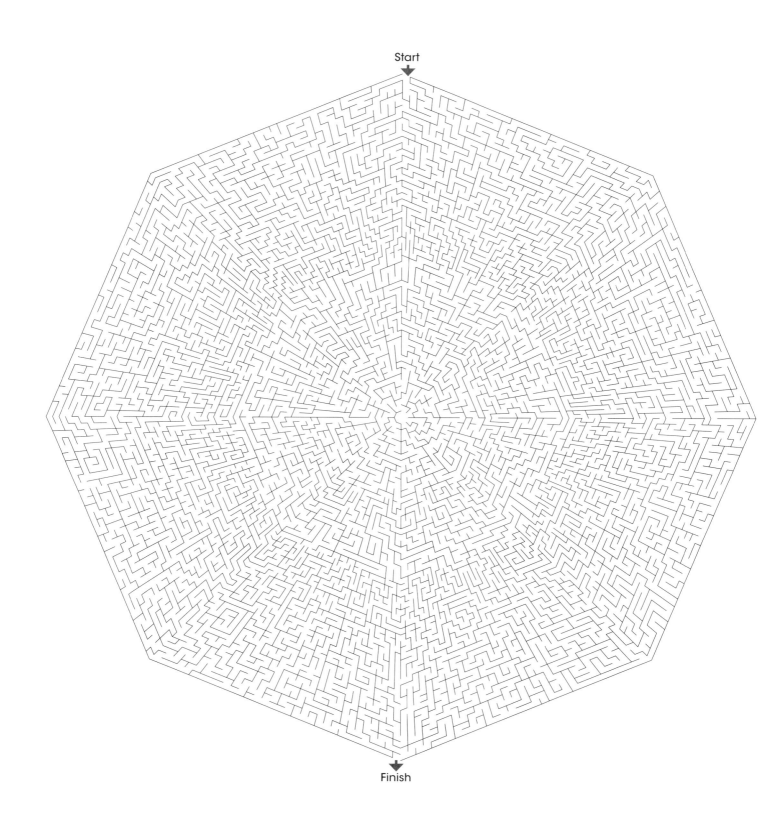

Finish

Start

Finish

Start

Finish

1 ●

2 ●

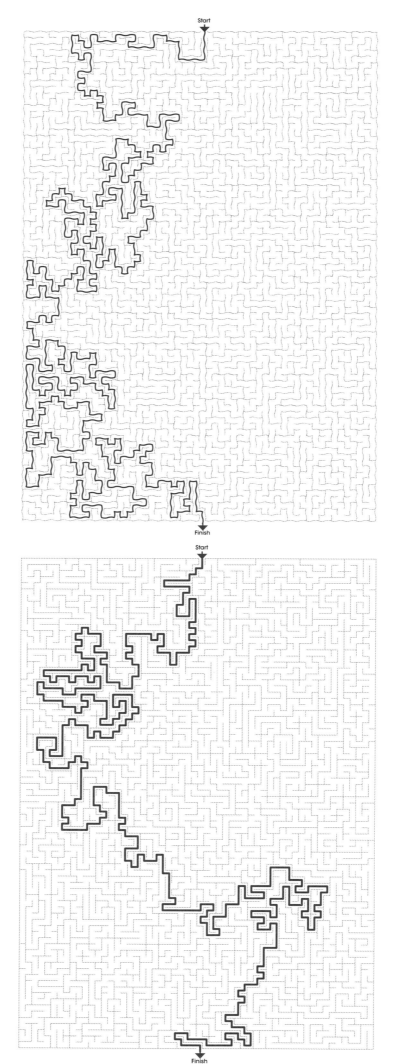

3 ●

Start

Finish

4 ●

Start

Finish

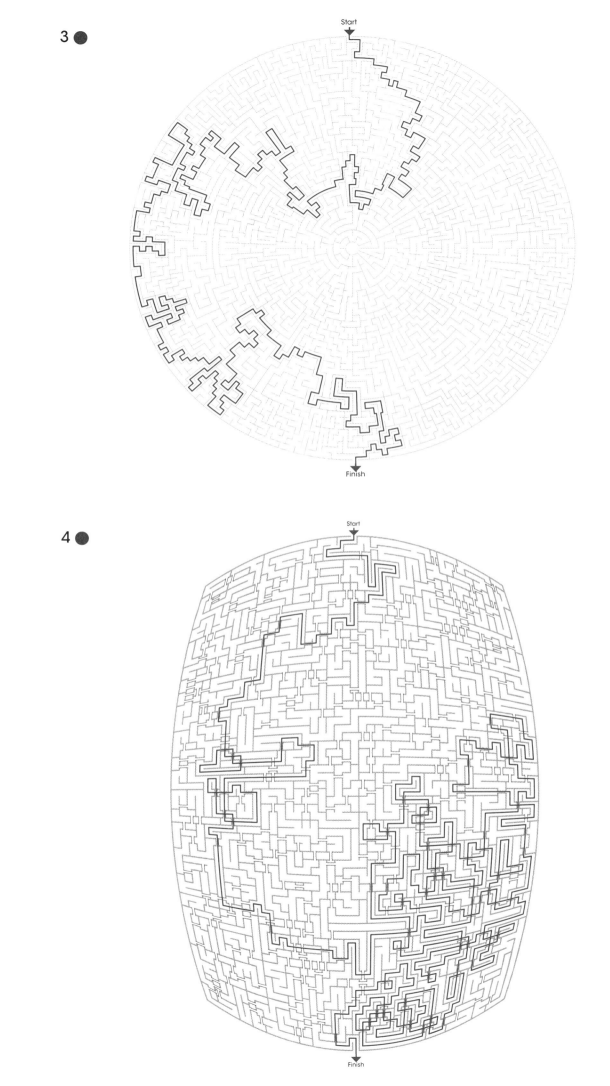

5 ●

6 ●

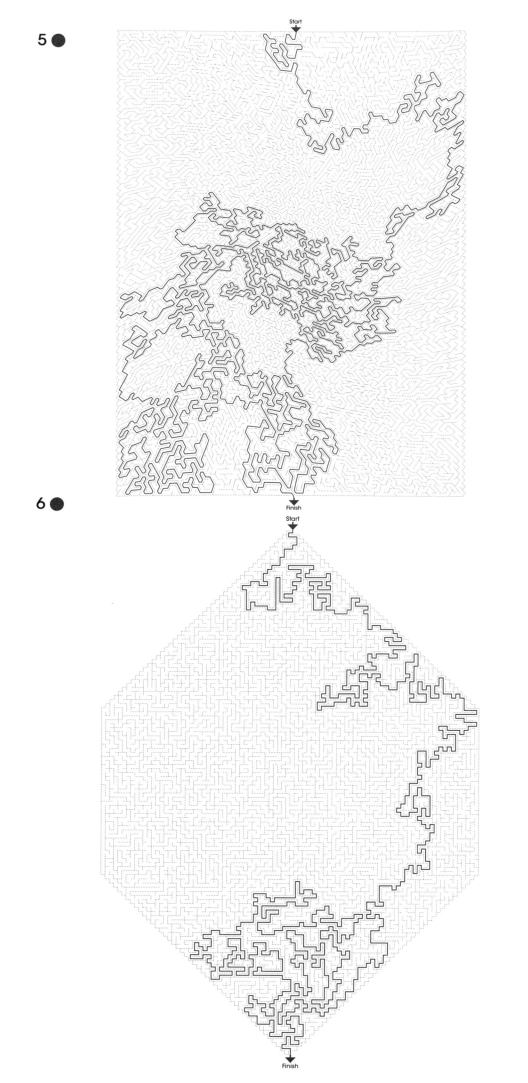

Start

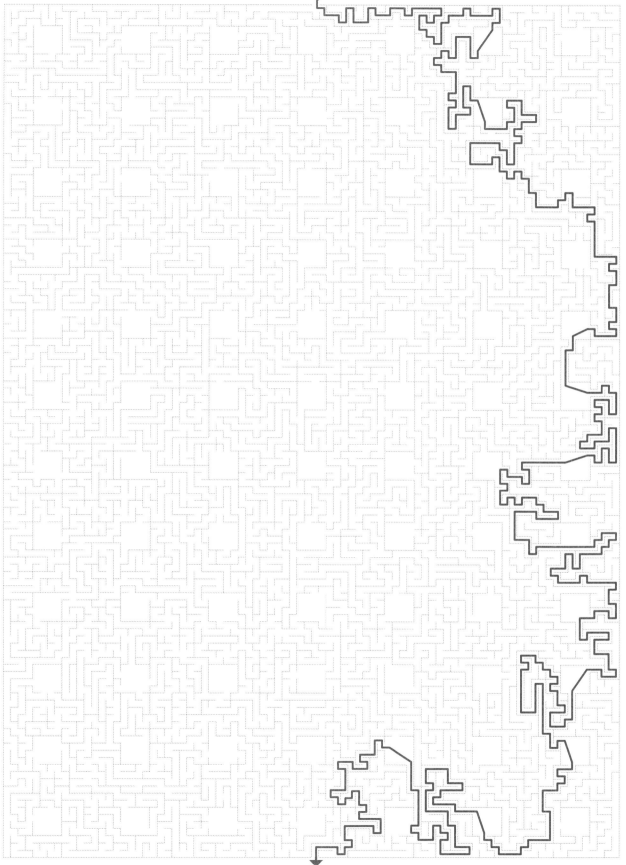

Finish

8 ●

Start

Finish

9 ●

10 ●

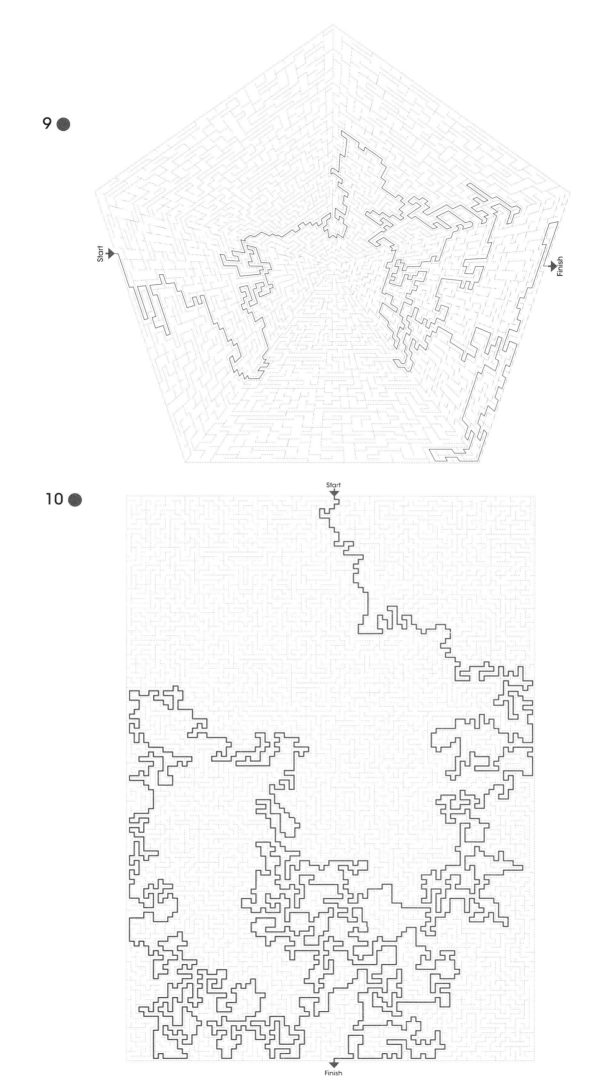

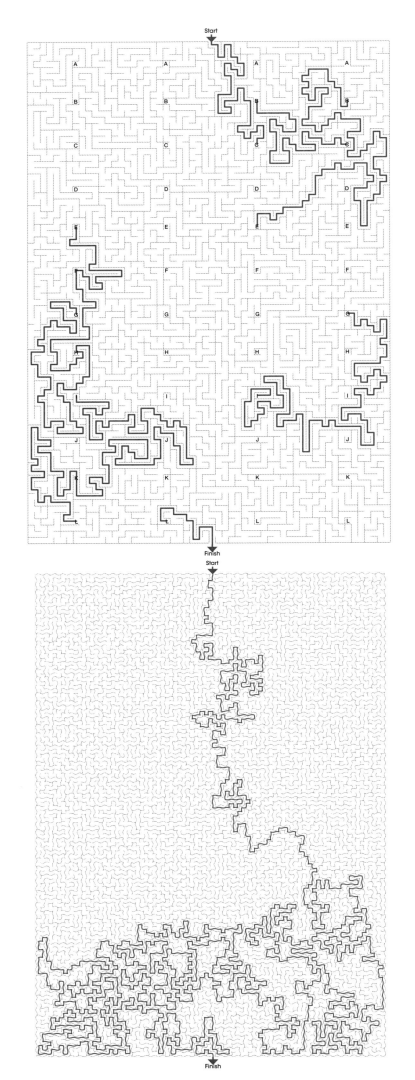

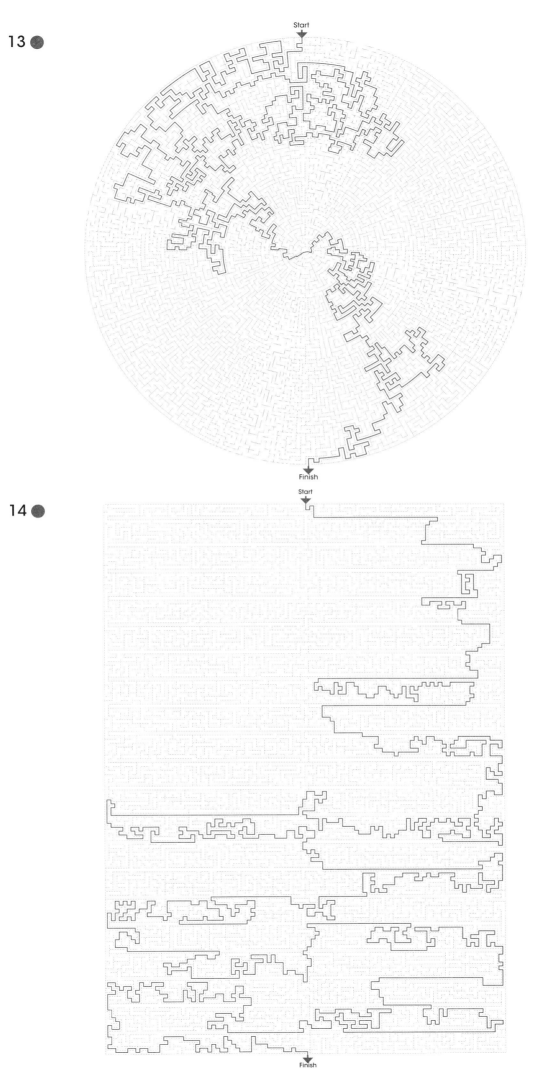

13 ●

Start

Finish

14 ●

Start

Finish

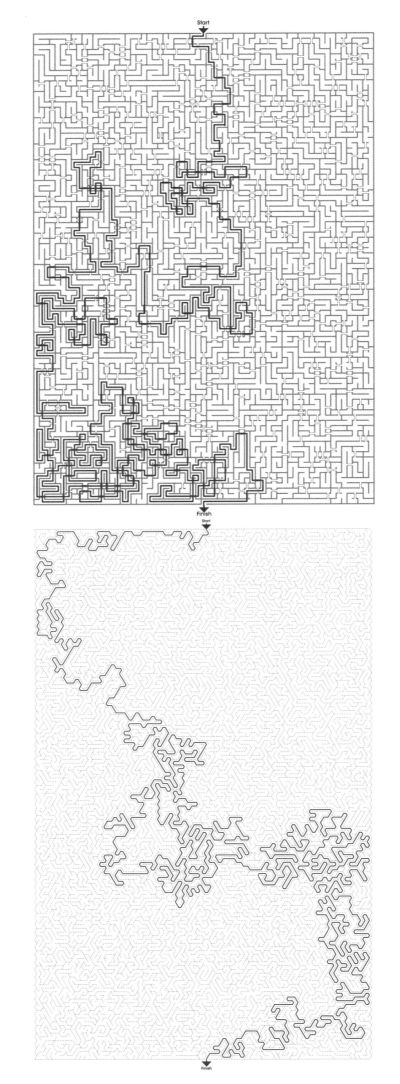

15

Start

Finish

16

Start

Finish

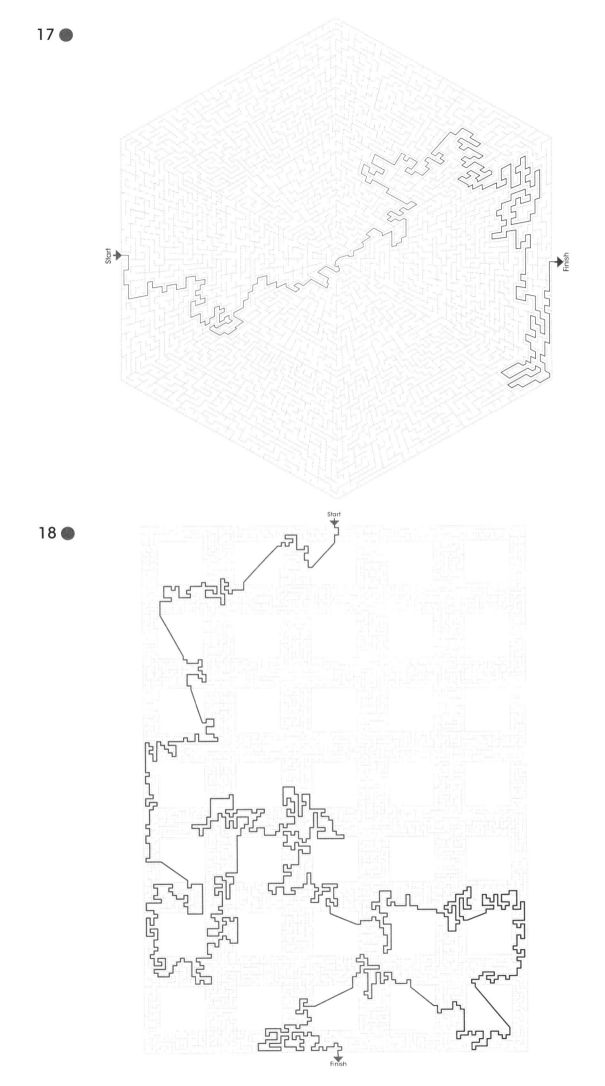

19 ⬤

Start

Finish

20 ⬤

Start

Finish

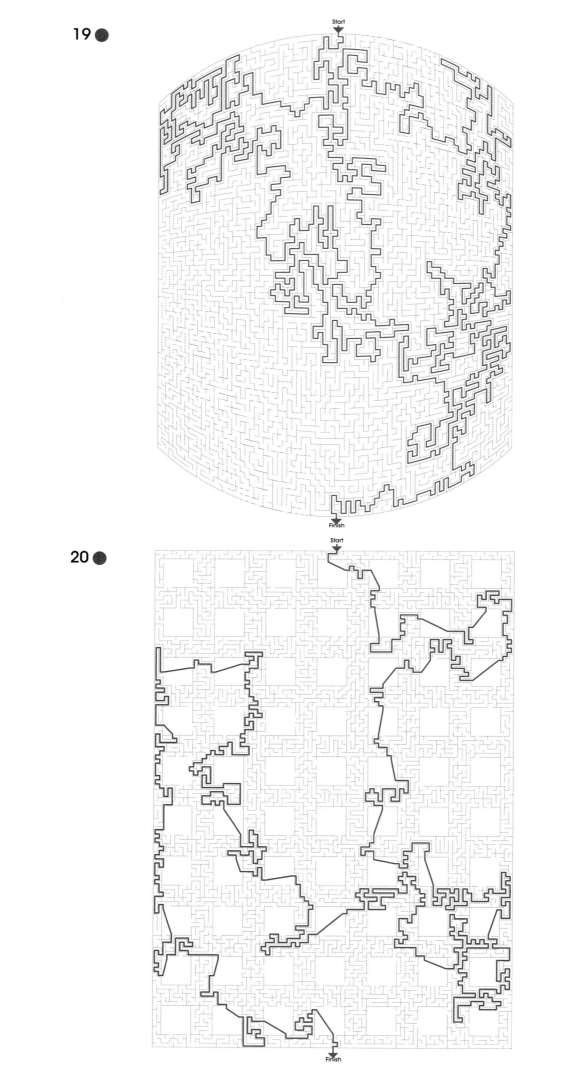

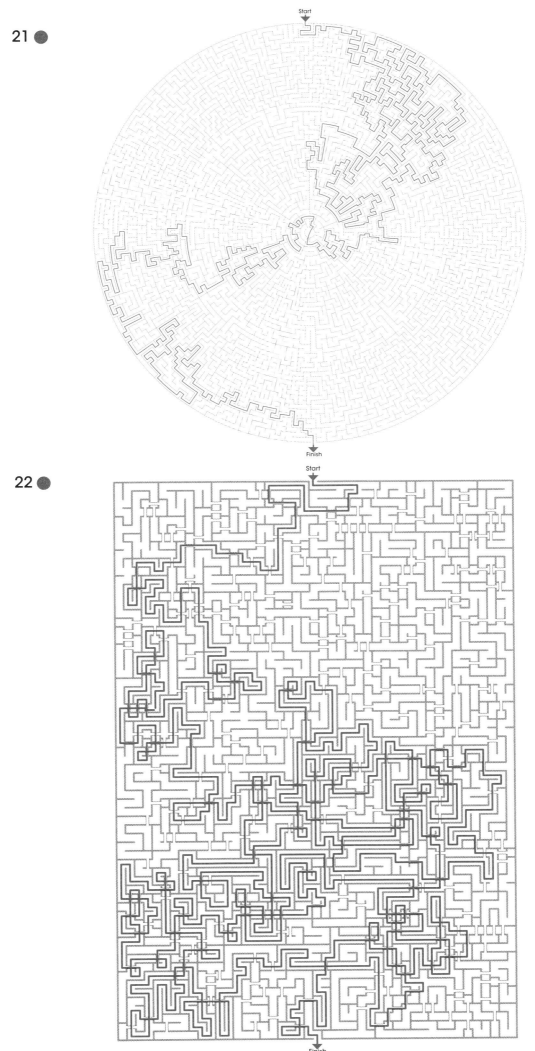

21 ●

22 ●

23 ●

Start

Finish

24 ●

Start

Finish

Start

Finish

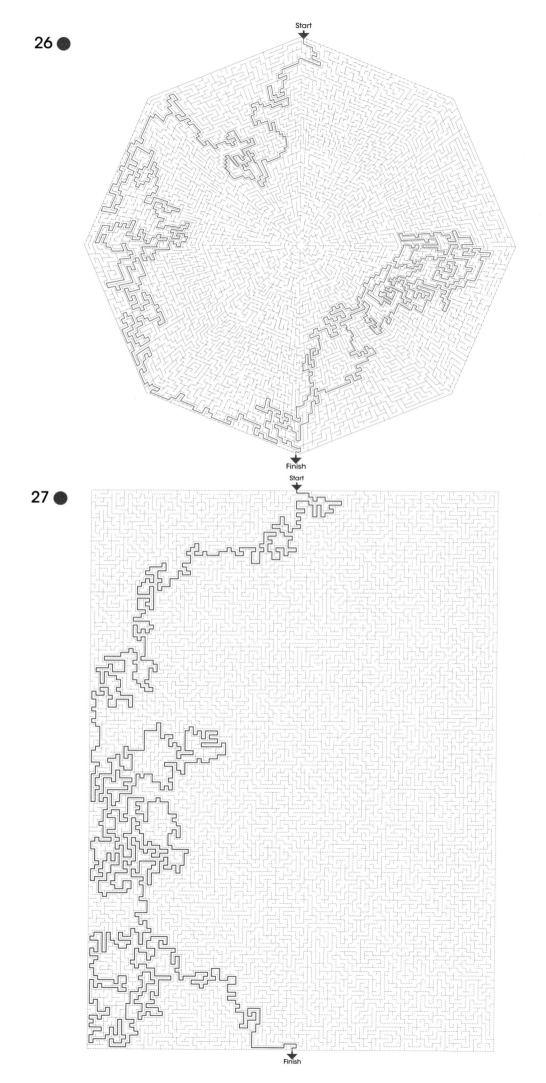

26 ●

Start

Finish

27 ●

Start

Finish

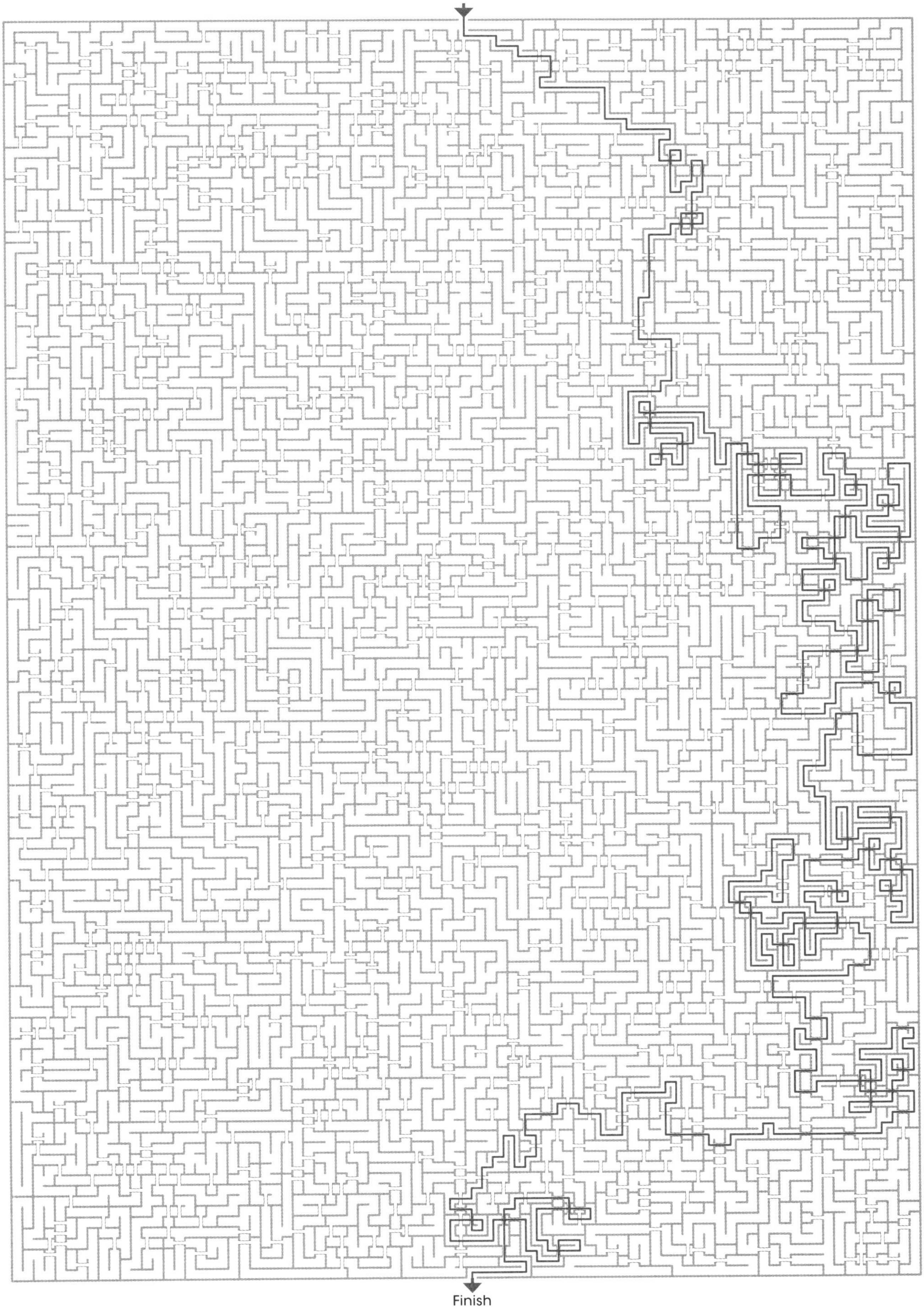
Finish

Start

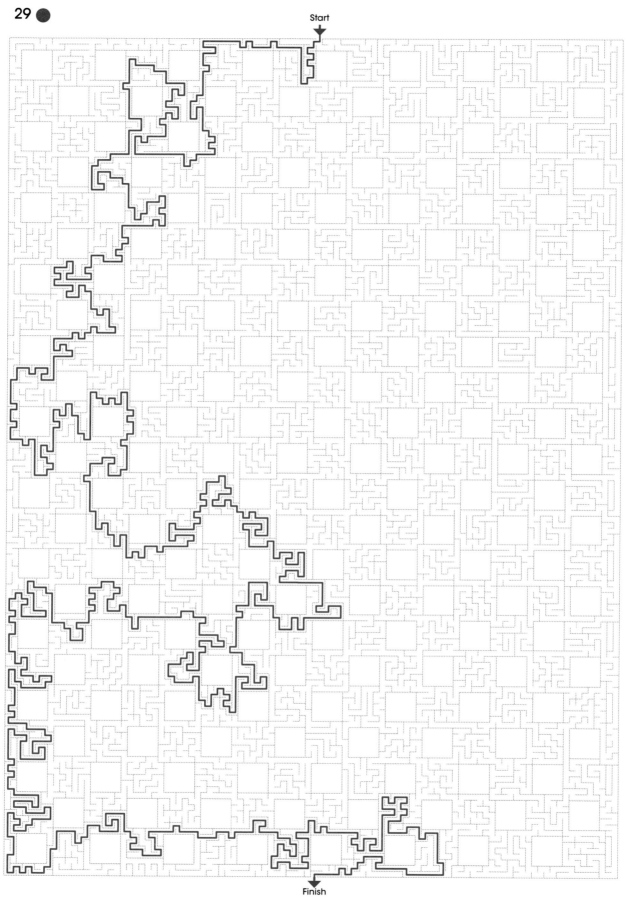

Finish

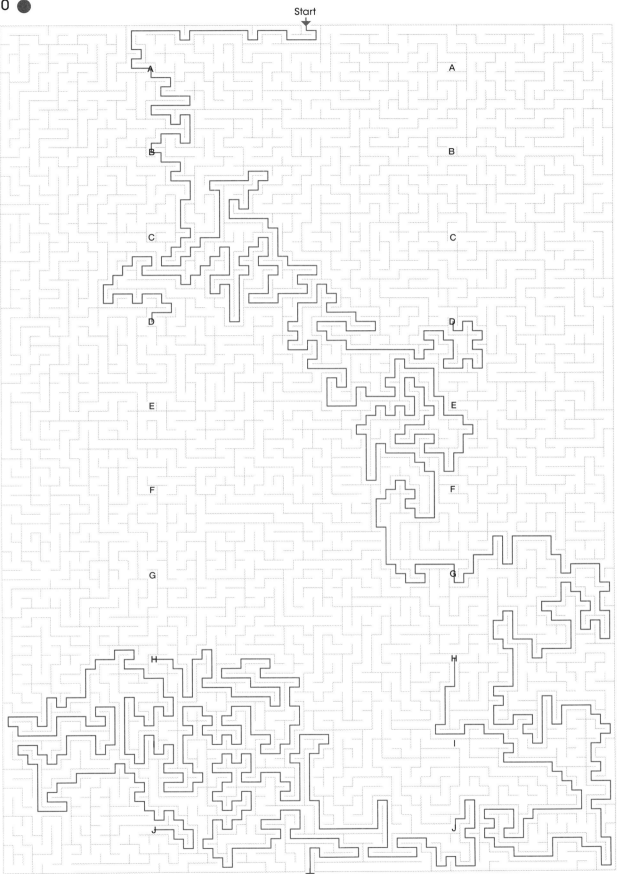

Dr Gareth Moore B.Sc (Hons) M.Phil Ph.D is the
author of over 50 puzzle and brain-training books
for both children and adults, including *Anti-Stress
Puzzles*, *Ultimate Dot to Dot* and *Brain Games
for Clever Kids*. He is the creator of the daily
brain-training website BrainedUp.com and runs
popular puzzle site PuzzleMix.com. He also
frequently appears in the media as a
puzzle expert.

First published in Great Britain in 2023 by Michael O'Mara Books Limited,
9 Lion Yard, Tremadoc Road, London SW4 7NQ

Edited by Hannah Daffern
Designed by Zoe Bradley

The material in this book previously appeared in *Ultimate Mazes* and *Extreme Mazes*

W www.mombooks.com   f Michael O'Mara Books   🐦 @OMaraBooks   📷 @omarabooks

Puzzle copyright © Gareth Moore 2016, 2017, 2023

www.drgarethmoore.com

All rights reserved. No part of this book may be reproduced, stored in a
retrieval system, or transmitted in any form or by any means, without the
prior permission in writing of the publisher, nor be otherwise circulated in
any form of binding or cover other than that in which it is published and
without a similar condition including this condition being imposed
on the subsequent purchaser.

A CIP catalogue record for this book is available
from the British Library.

ISBN: 978-1-78929-612-9

1 3 5 7 9 10 8 6 4 2

This book was printed in China.

MIX
Paper from
responsible sources
FSC® C020056
FSC
www.fsc.org